LEVEL
3
Fact Reader

Roar!

100 FUN Facts About African Animals

Stephanie Warren Drimmer

NATIONAL
GEOGRAPHIC

Washington, D.C.

For the littlest Hankins —S.W.D.

Trade paperback ISBN: 978-1-4263-3241-8
Reinforced library binding ISBN: 978-1-4263-3242-5

Designed by Yay! Design

The author and publisher gratefully acknowledge the expert content review of this book by Jef Dupain, VP of Programs, Central and West Africa, African Wildlife Foundation; Becca Van Beek, curator of Africa and Primates, Oregon Zoo; and Bob Lee, animal curator and elephant manager, Oregon Zoo; and the literacy review of this book by Mariam Jean Dreher, professor of reading education, University of Maryland, College Park.

Photo Credits

Cover, Michael Duva/Getty Images; 1, Yva Momatiuk and John Eastcott/Minden Pictures; 3, Anan Kaewkhammul/Shutterstock; 4 (UP), nattanan726/Shutterstock; 4 (CTR LE), Robert Harding Picture Library/National Geographic Creative; 4 (CTR RT), fivespots/Shutterstock; 4-5, Eric Isselée/Shutterstock; 5 (UP), johan63/Getty Images; 5 (CTR LE), tanuha2001/Shutterstock; 5 (CTR CTR), Nick Garbutt/Nature Picture Library; 5 (CTR RT), Yvette Cardozo/Getty Images; 5 (LO LE), WebSubstance/Getty Images; 6, Russell Burden/Getty Images; 7 (UP), Volodymyr Burdiak/Shutterstock; 7 (LO), Tony Wood/Science Source; 8, squashedbox/Getty Images; 9 (UP), ANDREYGUDKOV/Getty Images; 9 (LO), StuPorts/Getty Images; 10, Simon Eeman/Shutterstock; 12 (UP), Dave Watts/Nature Picture Library; 12 (LO), Thomas Dressler/Getty Images; 13 (UP), Marion Vollborn/Minden Pictures; 13 (CTR), Howard Klaaste/Shutterstock; 13 (LO), Martin Mecnarowski/Shutterstock; 14 (LE), Goncalo Diniz/Alamy Stock Photo; 14-15, hphimagelibrary/Getty Images; 15 (UP), Richard Du Toit/Nature Picture Library; 15 (LO), Tom Nebbia/Getty Images; 16 (UP), Paul Souders/Getty Images; 16 (LO), Victoria Stone & Mark Deeble/Getty Images; 17 (UP), Ilza/Getty Images; 17 (LO), David Havel/Shutterstock; 18-19, WLDavies/Getty Images; 20, Danita Delimont/Getty Images; 21 (UP), Mary Ann McDonald/Shutterstock; 21 (LO), Suzi Eszterhas/Minden Pictures; 22 (LE), Eric Isselée/Shutterstock; 22 (RT), Jak Wonderly; 23 (UP), Thomas Marent/Minden Pictures; 23 (CTR), Anup Shah/Nature Picture Library; 23 (LO), Nagel Photography/Shutterstock; 24, lilly3/Getty Images; 25 (UP), Denis-Huot/Nature Picture Library; 25 (LO), Thomas Marent/Minden Pictures; 26 (UP), Jen Guyton/Nature Picture Library; 26-27, Nigel Dennis/Getty Images; 27 (LE), Kit Korzun/Shutterstock; 27 (CTR), Independent birds/Shutterstock; 27 (RT), Morgan Trimble/Getty Images; 28-29, Martin Dohrn/Nature Picture Library; 29 (LE), Emil Von Maltitz/Getty Images; 29 (RT), Theo Webb/Nature Picture Library; 30-31, Vaganundo_Che/Shutterstock; 32, jez_bennett/Getty Images; 33, Utopia_88/Getty Images; 34, Roland Seitre/Minden Pictures; 35 (UP), LouisLotterPhotography/Shutterstock; 35 (CTR), Frans Lanting/National Geographic Creative; 35 (LO), Solvin Zankl/Nature Picture Library; 36, Divepic/Getty Images; 37, Anolis01/Getty Images; 38, Four Oaks/Shutterstock; 39, simplytheyu/Getty Images; 40, IMAGEMORE Co, Ltd./Getty Images; 41 (UP), Krotovych Oleh/Shutterstock; 41 (LO), FLPA/Alamy Stock Photo; 42-43, Yva Momatiuk and John Eastcott/Minden Pictures; 44 (UP), Enjoylife2/Getty Images; 44 (CTR LE), Trevor Frost/National Geographic Creative; 44 (CTR RT), Eric Isselée/Shutterstock; 44 (LO), Martin Harvey/Getty Images; 45 (UP LE), Jason Prince/Shutterstock; 45 (UP RT), GrigoryL/Shutterstock; 45 (CTR LE), Johan Swanepoel/Shutterstock; 45 (CTR RT), Be Good/Shutterstock; 45 (LO LE), USO/Getty Images; 45 (LO RT), fmajor/Getty Images; header (throughout), practicuum/Shutterstock

National Geographic supports K–12 educators with ELA Common Core Resources. Visit natgeoed.org/commoncore for more information.

Printed in the United States of America
19/WOR/2

Table of Contents

1
Leopards are good swimmers.

2
Rhinos have poor eyesight—sometimes they attack trees and rocks by accident!

3
The venomous puff adder kills more humans than any other snake in Africa.

4
Springboks like to jump in the air over and over. It's called "pronking," and scientists aren't sure why they do it.

5
Some of Africa's tree seeds have to be swallowed and pooped out by elephants before they can sprout.

6
African elephants have the largest ears of any animal in the world.

7
Hyenas live in groups of up to 80 individuals.

8
Sand cats have thick fur on their paws that helps protect them from hot desert sand.

9
Lions in a pride say hello by rubbing their heads together.

25 COOL FACTS ABOUT AFRICAN

10
At birth, a giraffe is the height of an adult man.

11
A male African elephant's tusks can be eight feet long. That's longer than a king-size bed!

12
A zebra's stripes are as unique as your fingerprint. No two zebras have the same pattern of stripes.

13
Hyenas look like dogs, but they're more closely related to cats.

14
African elephants create about 200 pounds of poop a day. That's as much as a refrigerator weighs!

15
A Darwin's bark spider can spin a web 82 feet across—about as long as two city buses!

16
Civets produce a substance that was once used as an ingredient in perfume.

17
A leopard's hearing is five times better than a human's hearing.

18
Sociable weaverbirds build nests that can be 20 feet wide and have 100 or more nesting chambers.

19
An impala's leap can carry it 30 feet—about the length of a city bus!

21
Giraffes' tongues are blue-black to protect them from sunburn.

20
Male African kudus grow spiral-shaped horns.

22
An ostrich's eyes are about the size of racquetballs.

23
Leopards are so strong they can drag an animal twice their weight up a tree.

24
Buffalo will chase lions that have attacked a member of their herd.

25
A giraffe's neck can be eight feet long—but it has the same number of neck bones as a human: seven.

ANIMALS

CHAPTER 1

THE ANIMALS OF AFRICA

Africa is home to some of the BIGGEST, TALLEST, FASTEST, AND MOST DANGEROUS animals on Earth.

The African elephant is the world's HEAVIEST LAND ANIMAL.

The world's SMALLEST BUTTERFLY is the dwarf blue.

When the orange sun rises over Africa, many animals come out to eat breakfast. Giraffes stretch their long necks to nibble tender leaves. Elephants sip water through their bendy trunks. Antelopes gather to graze while lions lazily look on. All kinds of creatures make their home here.

grassland

A biome is a large area on Earth that has its own weather and its own plants and animals.

When you think of Africa, you probably think of the long, waving grasses of the savanna. But Africa has three major biomes where different plants and animals live.

Almost half of Africa is savanna, a grassland dotted with trees. In the rain forest, lots of rain means everything is green. In the desert, few plants grow because water is scarce.

rain forest

Half of Africa's animals LIVE IN RAIN FORESTS.

The entire United States could FIT INSIDE AFRICA'S LARGEST DESERT, the Sahara.

desert

CHAPTER 2

IN THE GRASSLAND

A lion's roar can be heard FIVE MILES AWAY.

USUALLY, ALL THE LIONESSES IN A PRIDE ARE RELATED—they are each other's mothers, daughters, grandmothers, and granddaughters.

The lion is called the "king of beasts" for a reason. These fearsome cats chase down large animals like zebras and wildebeests. But even though the males look fiercer, it's the females that do most of the hunting. That's because male lions can be as heavy as 420 pounds. The females are lighter and more nimble, which makes them natural hunters.

Lions live in groups called prides. A pride can have up to 30 lions that share a close bond. The lions work together to hunt and raise the cubs. When they grow up, male cubs usually go off to form their own prides. Females often stay in their mother's pride for life.

The lion isn't the only cat that plays and pounces on the savanna. Here are a few more of the African savanna's fantastic felines.

BLACK-FOOTED CAT: This is the smallest wild cat in Africa. Some grow to just 2.4 pounds!

CHEETAH: The fastest land animal on Earth, this cat can run up to 60 or perhaps even 70 miles an hour.

A cheetah can pick up speed FASTER THAN MOST CARS.

CARACAL: These cat acrobats can catch multiple birds in one leap.

SERVAL: This expert pouncer can leap 12 feet to snag its prey.

AFRICAN WILDCAT: This kitty is the ancestor of our modern pet cats.

13

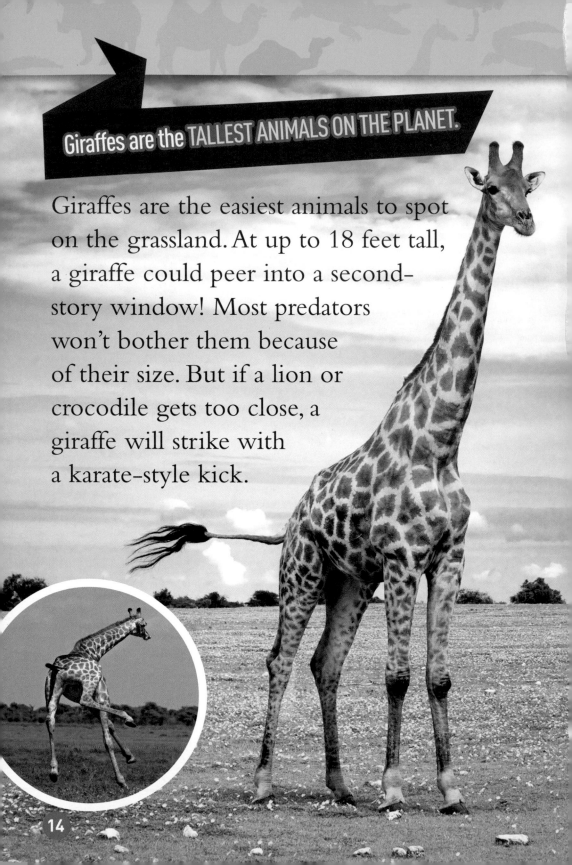

Giraffes are the easiest animals to spot on the grassland. At up to 18 feet tall, a giraffe could peer into a second-story window! Most predators won't bother them because of their size. But if a lion or crocodile gets too close, a giraffe will strike with a karate-style kick.

Most people think giraffes
don't make noise. But they do!
Giraffes make several sounds,
including a humming sound
that's so low, it's hard for
humans to hear. When they
sense danger, they snort. Then
the whole herd takes off
running. Other animals on the
savanna use giraffes as their
alarm system. If the giraffes
start running, they do, too!

Giraffes
snack on leaves
for 16 TO 20 HOURS
A DAY.

Pool Party

An elephant's tusks NEVER STOP GROWING.

Elephants can breathe while underwater BY USING THEIR TRUNKS LIKE A SNORKEL.

Elephants love to cool off in the savanna's lakes and rivers. But they're not the only African animals that enjoy a refreshing dip.

HIPPO: These big bathers are adapted for life in the water. Their eyes, ears, and nostrils poke above the surface while their bodies are underwater. Hippos sometimes nap underwater— but they can't swim!

A group of rhinos IS CALLED A CRASH.

RHINO: Rhinos' thick skin is surprisingly sensitive. These animals plunge into lakes and rivers to coat themselves in mud. It protects them from sun and insect bites.

CROCODILE: *Snap!* These huge river dwellers can be 20 feet long. They mostly eat fish, but they will attack anything that comes too close. That includes zebras, birds—and even other crocodiles.

NILE CROCODILES CAN WEIGH UP TO 1,650 POUNDS—as much as a large horse!

Road Trip

About 1.5 million wildebeests migrate MORE THAN 1,800 MILES EACH YEAR.

Africa's grazers are always on the move. Every year, huge herds of wildebeests, zebras, and antelope travel across East Africa in search of fresh grass.

WILDEBEESTS CAN RUN WITHIN MINUTES after they are born.

Predators like lions and hyenas follow close behind. They're on the hunt for an easy meal. This amazing event is called the Great Migration.

People travel from all over the world to catch a glimpse of the animals making their long journey.

Oxpecker birds ride on the backs of wildebeests and other large grazers. THE BIRDS SNACK ON BUGS THEY FIND IN THE FUR.

CHAPTER 3

IN THE RAIN FOREST

An adult male gorilla eats about 40 POUNDS OF FOOD A DAY.

A gorilla's daily schedule is eating, sleeping, and more eating! When a troop of mountain gorillas wakes up in the morning, it's time for breakfast. An adult male, called a silverback, leads the group. He brings the troop to a feeding spot, where they spend the morning munching on plants. Then it's naptime.

SILVERBACKS POUND THEIR CHESTS to show other gorillas they're in charge.

Young gorillas spend their days playing—JUST LIKE HUMAN CHILDREN!

A BABY GORILLA CLINGS TO ITS MOTHER'S BELLY FUR and never leaves mom for the first few months.

Each adult gorilla weaves branches into a nest. They climb inside for a snooze while the youngsters play. After the gorillas wake up, they eat again until bedtime, when it's time to make another nest. Gorillas rarely use the same nest twice.

Gorillas are just one of the many primates that make their home in Africa's rain forest.

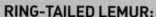

RING-TAILED LEMUR:
These forest dwellers live only on Africa's largest island, Madagascar. The black-and-white rings on their tails help other lemurs spot them. A ring-tailed lemur's tail is longer than its body!

A male MANDRILL'S COLORFUL FACE helps him attract females.

COLOBUS MONKEY: Colobus monkeys spend nearly their whole lives up high in the trees. They leap from branch to branch, sometimes dropping as much as 50 feet to a branch below.

COMMON CHIMPANZEE: Along with bonobos, they're humans' closest living relatives. Like us, they use tools: Chimps use rocks as hammers to crack open nuts. They also use twigs to fish termites out of nests.

Mangabeys have SPECIAL THROAT SACS that give them booming voices.

Hard to Spot

Unlike their giant cousins, PYGMY HIPPOS RUN AND HIDE WHEN THREATENED.

Some rain forest animals are so shy that humans almost never see them in the wild. Pygmy hippos are good at hiding in the thick jungle. Forest elephants move almost silently. Since they're so hard to find, scientists know very little about these mysterious animals.

Pygmy hippos are about THREE FEET TALL.

The Congo peacock, another shy rain forest animal, SINGS IN DUETS.

At night, goliath frogs come out to look for food. At more than a foot long and weighing up to 7.2 pounds, they are AS BIG AS SOME HOUSE CATS!

AN OKAPI'S TONGUE IS 18 INCHES LONG and can reach into its ears.

leaf-tailed gecko

Other rain forest animals are tough to find because they use camouflage (KAM-uh-flahj) to stay hidden. The okapi's stripes help it blend in with the forest. Leaf-tailed geckos look like part of the tree they rest on. Camouflage helps keep these animals safe from predators.

Pangolins CURL UP INTO SCALY BALLS to protect themselves from lions and leopards.

Is it a pinecone with legs? An artichoke with eyes? No, it's a pangolin, another hard-to-find rain forest animal! This odd creature uses its long, sticky tongue to lick up insects. One pangolin can slurp down 20,000 ants in a single day!

Pangolins have hard scales that make them almost invincible. But humans hunt them for their meat and scales. Pangolins are just one of Africa's rain forest animals that are in danger of disappearing.

Pangolins **DON'T HAVE TEETH.** Spines in their stomach help grind up food.

Pangolins are the ONLY MAMMALS WITH SCALES.

ANIMALS AT RISK
Many animals across Africa are endangered.

CROSS RIVER GORILLA: Humans have moved into their forests. Fewer than 300 are left on Earth.

AFRICAN GRAY PARROT: These birds are as smart as a five-year-old child. They're captured to be sold as pets.

PICKERSGILL'S REED FROG: The habitat of this bright green frog has shrunk to just 3.5 square miles.

Small but Deadly

One of a pangolin's favorite foods is army ants. Few creatures are brave enough to eat them—because they'll bite back! Army ants can be almost one inch long. Their snapping jaws are bigger than their whole head!

The tiny mosquito is the MOST DANGEROUS ANIMAL in the entire world. Mosquitoes carry diseases that kill several million people each year.

Unlike other ants, army ants don't build underground burrows. Instead, they spend their lives on the move. And when they move, every animal around better watch out. They head out to find food in groups of more than 100,000. Though they're not dangerous to humans, they tear apart and eat everything from scorpions to small reptiles!

CHAPTER 4

IN THE DESERT

THE OSTRICH is the world's tallest and heaviest bird.

OSTRICHES HOLD OUT THEIR WINGS for balance when they run.

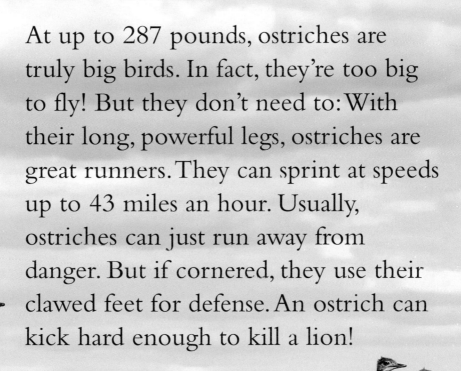

At up to 287 pounds, ostriches are truly big birds. In fact, they're too big to fly! But they don't need to: With their long, powerful legs, ostriches are great runners. They can sprint at speeds up to 43 miles an hour. Usually, ostriches can just run away from danger. But if cornered, they use their clawed feet for defense. An ostrich can kick hard enough to kill a lion!

Eating one ostrich egg would be like eating 24 CHICKEN EGGS.

One pack of African painted dogs can occupy a territory BIGGER THAN LOS ANGELES.

Each morning, African painted dogs gear up for the hunt. They leap and play, letting out excited chirps and yips. These animals are among the best hunters in Africa. They catch their prey about eight times out of ten. That makes them more than twice as successful as lions!

Painted dogs work together to hunt. Using their large ears, they signal which direction the pack will go. They also communicate with sounds, such as twitters, barks, and rumbles.

PAINTED DOGS HUNT BY OUTRUNNING THEIR PREY. They can run up to 37 miles an hour for three miles. That's faster than a horse!

Some experts think painted dogs SNEEZE TO "VOTE" on group decisions.

Heat Wave

Camels can go for SIX MONTHS without drinking water.

They manage this feat by living off energy stores in their humps. And they're not the only animals with bodies built to survive in the African desert.

Some African animals, like kangaroo rats, NEVER NEED TO DRINK WATER AT ALL. They get all they need from their food.

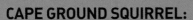

CAPE GROUND SQUIRREL: This rodent holds its fluffy tail over its head—like an umbrella! It's not for rain, though. The tail provides shade from the hot sun.

SAND GROUSE: This bird's feathers are like sponges. Males will fly to a nearby pond, soak up some water, and head back to the nest to share with their partners.

FOGSTAND BEETLE: This insect stands totally still as the morning fog washes over the sand in the Namib Desert. When the water collects as droplets, the beetle gets a drink.

Cuteness Contest

Rock hyrax: The rock hyrax (HI-raks) isn't a rodent. It's a relative of the elephant! Look closely and you might notice two tiny tusks. These furry critters live in colonies of up to 50. During the day, they like to sunbathe, and at night, they all cuddle up together. Aww!

ROCK HYRAXES HAVE FEET LIKE SUCTION CUPS that help them cling to rocks.

Fennec fox: The smallest of all the world's foxes, fennec foxes weigh just a little more than two pounds. Their thick, soft fur protects them from the hot sun during the day. Their huge ears look like they're too big for the fox's body! Their ears help keep them cool. They give off heat and lower the body temperature of these desert dwellers.

Fennec foxes can leap A DISTANCE OF FOUR FEET.

Dung beetles are found on EVERY CONTINENT EXCEPT ANTARCTICA.

Dung beetles can move dung balls 50 TIMES THEIR OWN WEIGHT.

Dung beetles USE THE MILKY WAY TO NAVIGATE. They are the first known animals to do this.

Not all of Africa's desert animals are cute! This hot home is also shared by a not-so-adorable animal: the dung beetle. Dung beetles get their name because they shape bits of dung, or animal poop, into balls. They use their superstrong front legs to roll the dung balls away and bury them. Then, female dung beetles use them as a place to lay their eggs. When the baby beetles are born, the dung becomes their first meal.

They might seem gross, but dung beetles are the planet's cleanup crew. If it weren't for them, huge parts of the Earth would be covered with millions of tons of dung!

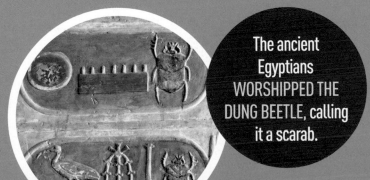

The ancient Egyptians WORSHIPPED THE DUNG BEETLE, calling it a scarab.

Desert Dangers

The smaller a scorpion's pincers, or front claws, THE STRONGER ITS VENOM.

Some of Africa's most dangerous animals LIVE IN ITS DESERTS.

Deathstalker scorpion: This stealthy stinger has the strongest venom of any scorpion. If stung, a person may experience extreme pain, paralysis, and even death.

Sand viper: This sneaky snake wiggles itself into the desert sand until just its eyes peek out. Then it waits to grab its prey. It mostly eats small mammals, birds, and reptiles, but its bite is dangerous to humans, too.

Desert crocodile: Crocs rarely go far from water. So scientists were shocked when they found some living on the edge of the Sahara in 2002. In the dry season, the animals enter a sleepy state. They barely eat or move for months until the rains come again.

DESERT CROCODILES ARE TINY—only about five feet long, compared to a Nile croc's 16 feet.

Animals eat, sleep, and play across Africa's many landscapes. Wildebeests kick up dust as their huge herds move across the grassland. Baby gorillas tumble on the rain forest floor. Nearby, their parents nap.

Fennec foxes swivel their big ears. They're listening to ostriches galloping across the desert sand. And when mighty lions roar, their voices echo across the savanna. For all of these creatures, Africa is home.

1 Though they're sometimes nicknamed the "king of the jungle," lions live in deserts and grasslands.

2 If a baby ring-tailed lemur is orphaned, the rest of the troop will take care of it.

3 Cheetahs need to drink water only every three to four days.

4 African painted dogs can have up to 20 puppies in a litter.

5 An aardvark can eat 50,000 ants in one meal.

6

7 Some experts think humans used African camels to carry heavy loads as long as 6,000 years ago.

Baboons use at least 10 different sounds to "talk" to each other.

8 A camel's hump doesn't store water; it stores fat.

10 Chimps and bonobos have about 99 percent of the same DNA as humans.

9 Warthogs sometimes live in abandoned aardvark burrows.

25 MORE FACTS ABOUT AFRICAN

11 An elephant's trunk has 40,000 different muscles.

12 A rhino's horn is made of keratin, just like human hair and fingernails.

13 Zebra babies can run just an hour after they're born.

14 The word "rhinoceros" means "nose horn" in Latin.

15 Vultures often eat until they're too full to fly.

16 All of Africa's great apes are endangered.

17 A hyena can weigh 180 pounds—as much as an adult man.

18 Honey badgers are known for being fearless fighters. They will attack large or dangerous animals, such as cobras.

19 Meerkats build underground homes with multiple rooms and many exits.

20 The most dangerous large land animal in Africa is the hippo.

21 Hippos are closely related to whales.

22 Cape buffalo are strong enough to tip over a car.

23 A group of giraffes is called a tower.

24 Africa has penguins! They live on the continent's southwestern coast.

25 Mongooses can't be hurt by snake venom.

ANIMALS

AFRICAN ANIMAL FACTS ROUNDUP

ROAR!
You're king of the beasts in African animal knowledge. Did you catch all 100 facts?

1. Leopards are good swimmers. 2. Rhinos have poor eyesight—sometimes they attack trees and rocks by accident! 3. The venomous puff adder kills more humans than any other snake in Africa. 4. Springboks like to jump in the air over and over. It's called "pronking," and scientists aren't sure why they do it. 5. Some of Africa's tree seeds have to be swallowed and pooped out by elephants before they can sprout. 6. African elephants have the largest ears of any animal in the world. 7. Hyenas live in groups of up to 80 individuals. 8. Sand cats have thick fur on their paws that helps protect them from hot desert sand. 9. Lions in a pride say hello by rubbing their heads together. 10. At birth, a giraffe is the height of an adult man. 11. A male African elephant's tusks can be eight feet long. That's longer than a king-size bed! 12. A zebra's stripes are as unique as your fingerprint. No two zebras have the same pattern of stripes. 13. Hyenas look like dogs, but they're more closely related to cats. 14. African elephants create about 200 pounds of poop a day. That's as much as a refrigerator weighs! 15. A Darwin's bark spider can spin a web 82 feet across—about as long as two city buses! 16. Civets produce a substance that was once used as an ingredient in perfume. 17. A leopard's hearing is five times better than a human's hearing. 18. Sociable weaverbirds build nests that can be 20 feet wide and have 100 or more nesting chambers. 19. An impala's leap can carry it 30 feet—about the length of a city bus. 20. Male African kudus grow spiral-shaped horns. 21. Giraffes' tongues are blue-black to protect them from sunburn. 22. An ostrich's eyes are about the size of racquetballs. 23. Leopards are so strong they can drag an animal twice their weight up a tree. 24. Buffalo will chase lions that have attacked a member of their herd. 25. A giraffe's neck can be eight feet long—but it has the same number of neck bones as a human: seven. 26. Africa is home to some of the biggest, tallest, fastest, and most dangerous animals on Earth. 27. The African elephant is the world's heaviest land animal. 28. The world's smallest butterfly is the dwarf blue. 29. Half of Africa's animals live in rain forests. 30. The entire United States could fit inside Africa's largest desert, the Sahara. 31. A lion's roar can be heard five miles away. 32. Usually, all the lionesses in a pride are related—they are each other's mothers, daughters, grandmothers, and granddaughters. 33. The Swahili word for lion, *simba*, also means "king." 34. A cheetah can pick up speed faster than most cars. 35. Giraffes are the tallest animals on the planet. 36. Giraffes snack on leaves for 16 to 20 hours a day. 37. An elephant's tusks never stop growing. 38. Elephants can breathe while underwater by using their trunks like a snorkel. 39. A group of rhinos is called a crash. 40. Nile crocodiles can weigh up to 1,650 pounds—as much as a large horse. 41. About 1.5 million wildebeests migrate more than 1,800 miles each year. 42. Wildebeests can